Caudillismo
in
Latin America

Political and social
phenomena

Susana Rebon López

2nd. Edition

Author

Susana Rebon López

LinkedIn
https://www.linkedin.com/in/susanarebonlopez/

Twitter
https://twitter.com/srebon

The phenomenon of Latin American Caudillismo in the 19th century

... and that persists in the 21st century

CONTENT

o Caudillismo in   1

   Latin America

o Notes   32

o Sources   34

o Author   36

CAUDILLISMO IN LATIN AMERICA

The process of Independence is one of the essential factors that led to the appearance of the caudillo as a figure of power.

The vacuum of authority in vast geographical regions, such as the llanos of Venezuela and the pampas of Argentina, led to increased banditry, which took shape into impunity.

The members of these bands, skilled with weapons, obscene and cruel, and connoisseurs of the country, in the crucial moments of the struggles for independence, were captured to their ranks by both sides in a conflict.

In some cases, they were peons of the large farm or haciendas who, because of the disorder, had lost their masters others were simply adventurers or fugitive slaves, and there were also defectors of war. In any case, they were people who lived in a very hostile environment, which only survived in a group, and who, with their peculiar form of organization, offered a solution of order to the chaos at the moment.

A group with these characteristics always requires a leader. In this case, leadership characterized itself by strength, courage, audacity, a strong will, and fear that they were capable of instilling in its followers.

They were charismatic leaders by nature, were illiterate, and grew in very narrow contact with nature. They made decisions more intuitively than rational. They were telluric and visceral personalities, accommodated only to his will or to the of a stronger one. They were beings handed to passions, fond of women, the game of roosters and the bets, born seducers. The cities and their way of life adapted to the citizen norms were unknown to them. They lived and died practically in the same place where they were born.

It came out of this way as caudillo in Venezuela José Antonio Páez, and in Argentina, we have Facundo Quiroga. In Mexico emerges Santa Anna, who in this case comes from the regular army and is the son of a lawyer and colonial official. So, we can pose a possible hypothesis that more than a matter of upbringing or geographical determinism, it was a matter of indomitable personality, conditioned and valued by the circumstances of the war and conditions of peace. Most of them would only be in the best of cases, social misfits reluctant to any form of authority, or in an extreme case, very effective criminals.

In his Autobiography, José Antonio Páez tells us:

"Such was the life of those men. (...) The ringing of the bell that reminded them of religious duties never came to their ears, and they lived and died as men who had

no other destiny than to fight with the elements and beasts and their ambition was limited to one day to be a foreman in the same point where he had previously served in peon class." (1)

José Antonio Páez

They were men especially gifted physically to be able to resist and impose themselves in such a hostile environment. They copied somehow the ways of the beasts with which they shared the environment. The nicknames would refer to these. We have Paez called him the *Tigre de Payara* and Facundo the *Tigre de Los Llanos*, titles always won in actions of extreme violence, whether against the beasts or enemies of any kind, personal or political.

Facundo is described to us by Sarmiento:

"His black eyes full of fire and shaded by crowded eyebrows caused an

involuntary sensation of terror in those upon whom, sometimes they fixed because Facundo never looked at the front. And by habit, for art, for the desire of becoming fearsome, he had his head usually bowed and looked through his eyebrows (...)"
(2)

However, contrary to what one might think, they valued their way of life above what they assumed to be the citizens' way of life, which they perceived as weak. Many of these leaders only came to know them in the years when they gained Independence and served as support to hacendados and estancieros, who entered into politics wanted to assert their position against the city, or as in the case of Páez and Facundo when already generals directly assume government positions, national and provincial.

The perception of Páez is eloquent:

"The struggle of man with wild beasts -that are nothing more than horses and wild bulls- is a constant struggle in which life escapes as a miracle, a struggle that tests the body forces, and which needs moral resistance, much stoicism (...) That struggle, I say, had to be and was a terrible ordeal. (...) It was the gym where I acquired the athletic sturdiness that

was very useful to me many times later and that even today, men envy me in the vigor and strength of their years. My body by the force of blows became of iron, and my soul acquired, with the adversities in the first years, that temper that the most careful education could hardly have been able to give it.". (3)

Those who looked like this could hardly do anything but impose their forms on a community once they had the power to do so.

The confrontation between the values of the countryside and the city during the creation of the new nations is inevitable. Once the power granted by the victory in the War of Independence is in the hands of the caudillos, it will hardly yield to the politicians of the cities, or it can be subtracted to them by the civil power even though the reason based on the actions of these last. And it could not be otherwise.

Their actions were dictated by irrationality based on terror and own ignorance and the majority of the population.

"Facundo is a type of primitive barbarism: he did not know the subjection of any kind, his anger was that of the beasts (...) In the inability to handle the springs of civil government, he put terror as a record to replace patriotism and abnegation; ignorant, surrounded by mysteries and becoming impenetrable, using a natural sagacity, an uncommon ability to observe and the credulity of the plebe, pretended a prescience of events that gave him prestige and reputation among vulgar people." (4)

They embrace any political tendency, they can either support federalism or centralism as forms of government to be implemented, the one that favors them more personally, and they change their position when it is unfavorable to them; in any case, there is no other support in their decisions.

Facundo Quiroga

However, in almost all cases, if the city imposed the centralist regime, the regions rebelled because they did not feel represented in the decisions taken by the central power and therefore demanded that the government be the federal one.

In the case that the city advocated a federal government, the regional caudillos wanted to impose their position on each other, the federal government being unable to reconcile the positions found so that the strongest caudillo ventured into the city to force its policy, which generally proclaimed itself to be federalist in use, the action was typical of a central government.

In short, the regime that managed to impose itself in the first years of the life of the independent nations was the central conservative republican government, which after new fights, would give way to federal governments of liberal type.

Once they assume power, by force and terror, the caudillos take possession of the communal goods, monopolizing in their hands the principal sources of economic wealth of the region, which is below their government until decimate them in the majority of cases, which gave them the necessary goods to undertake the campaigns to gain power at the national level. Then, at the slightest excuse of warlike action they might undertake, the work of government delegates them to the most affectionate subordinate. They were men of war.

The network of relations that supported the power of the caudillos was established based on the friendship and compadrazgo between the leaders. They must know personally the individual to which they delegate. And their adherence had to be unconditional at the risk of losing personal wealth and life if they disagreed.

Antonio López de Santa Anna

Local and provincial caudillos are the basis of the power of the national caudillo within a pyramid organization. With subordinates, the relationship is from employer to client. In Venezuela, this relation derives from the one between the hacendado and the peon, and in Argentina, the estanciero and the gaucho. The patron protects and rewards the client according to their work and at the cost of a total adhesion. The caudillo rewarded them with lands or official positions to prey upon them. It depends on the moment.

After the Wars of Independence, the institutions of civic government disappeared, or they did not have the force to impose the norm and, for this reason, called to the caudillo. That is, in essence, its function. In the face of chaos, the autocratic order that would help to form the new national states is less evil.

"In taking power the caudillo usually followed a dual process: first he exercised informal authority and then actually took office as supreme executive, whether president or governor. But office did not replace a caudillo´s power or become a substitute for his authority: it simply

confirmed his position and reinforced his original capacity to take decisions and impose order, a capacity which he had won by his personal qualifications, his response to war, and his reaction to politics." (5)

Civil power would come later in Latin America, at the cost of the sacrifice and patience of the people. However, their permanence has not been stable. There are still states in Latin America that, although they call themselves democratic, are led by *de facto* national militarism.

The warrior society survives and continues to raise its values of domination and imposition of personalist policies by force above the value of reason and the conciliation and complementation of diverse positions, proper of civil society.

NOTES

1. José Antonio Páez, *Autobiografía*, Caracas, PDVSA, 1989. p.38.

2. Domingo F. Sarmiento, *Facundo*. Capítulo 5, Vida de Juan Facundo Quiroga.

3. José Antonio Páez, *Autobiografía*, Caracas, PDVSA, 1989. p.38.

4. Domingo F. Sarmiento, *Facundo*. Capítulo 5, Vida de Juan Facundo Quiroga.

5. John Lynch, *Caudillos in Spanish America. 1800-1850*, Oxford, Clarendon Press, 1992, p. 411.

SOURCES

HALPERING DONGHI, Tulio,

Historia Contemporánea de América Latina, Madrid, Alianza Editorial, 1972.

LYNCH, John,

Caudillos in Spanish America, 1800-1850, Oxford, Clarendon Press, 1992.

PÁEZ, José Antonio,
Autobiografía, Caracas, PDVSA, 1989.

PÉREZ GUILHOU, Dardo,
Presidencialismo, caudillismo y populismo.

SARMIENTO, Domingo F.,
Facundo.

ABOUT THE AUTHOR

Susana Rebon López

Mentor of the Leaders

Telecommunications Engineer

Bachelor of History

Universidad Central Venezuela, UCV.

Printed in Great Britain
by Amazon

18042649R00022